Scales Rule!

Seven Later Elementary Piano Solos
Based on Scales
by
Carolyn Miller

Contents

12148

Scaling the Walls
(C Major)

Allegro moderato

Carolyn Miller

Balancing the Scales
(G Major)

Carolyn Miller

Revised by David Engle

Miniature Scale
(F Major)

Moderato

Carolyn Miller

mf
f
L.H.
R.H.
L.H.

Scaling the Heights
(D Major)

With energy

Carolyn Miller

f
8va

Tipping the Scales

(A Major)

Carolyn Miller

Moderato

mf
8va

On a Scale of...

(B Major)

Carolyn Miller

f
cresc. poco a poco

A Graduated Scale
(E Major)

Moderato

Carolyn Miller

mf
f

f
mf
f